A Short and Easy Method of Prayer

Jeanne Marie Guyon

REJUVENATED BOOKS

Series One

A Short and Easy Method of Prayer
Rejuvenated Books: Series One
ISBN: 978-1-63171-004-9

Copyright ©2019 by Unorthodox Press. All rights reserved. Although the original text and many elderly English translations are now in the public domain, this rejuvenated paraphrase is a new creative work and fully protected by copyright law.

About this text: Jeanne-Marie Bouvier de la Motte Guyon, commonly referred to as Madame Guyon, was a wealthy French widow who practiced and promoted a form of Christian mysticism that became known as Quietism. First published in 1685, this work presents a short guide to this type of "quiet" prayer. It was the focal point for intense debate within the Catholic church and led to the author's imprisonment in 1689. It was later banned by the Catholic church but has nonetheless remained in print ever since. This paraphrase is based on third section of this volume:

> Fénelon, François and Madame Guyon. *Spiritual Progress: or Instructions in the Divine Life of the Soul.* Edited by James W. Metcalf. New York: M. W. Dodd, 1853.

This book is printed in the United States of America.

Contents

- » Preface 1
- » One: The Call to Prayer 7
- » Two: The First Level of Prayer 11
- » Three: Prayer without Reading 16
- » Four: The Second Level of Prayer 21
- » Five: Spiritual Droughts 24
- » Six: Abandonment 27
- » Seven: Suffering 31
- » Eight: Revelation 34
- » Nine: Virtue 37
- » Ten: Subduing the Body 39
- » Eleven: Conversion 43
- » Twelve: The Third Level of Prayer 47
- » Thirteen: The Presence of God 53
- » Fourteen: Inward Silence 55
- » Fifteen: Confession 58
- » Sixteen: Reading and Spoken Prayers 63
- » Seventeen: Requests 65

- » Eighteen: Failings.................... 67
- » Nineteen: Temptation 69
- » Twenty: The Death of Self 71
- » Twenty-one: Depending on the Spirit 76
- » Twenty-two: The Work of the Soul....... 89
- » Twenty-three: Guidance for Leaders...... 98
- » Twenty-four: Union with God 106

Walk before me, and be blameless. —Genesis 17.1

Preface

This little book, written in great simplicity, was not originally intended for publication. It was written to help a few individuals who desired to love God with their whole hearts. Because of the benefits they received from reading the manuscript, many of these asked to have copies of it. For this reason alone, it is committed to publication.

It remains in its original simplicity. It contains no judgments of the various divine leadings of others. On the contrary, it reinforces the received teachings of the church. I submit the whole to judgment of the learned and experienced, but with the request that they do not stop at the surface but consider my main purpose, which is to encourage and enable the world to love God and serve him with encouragement and success, offering a simple and easy method that is adapted for those little ones who are not qualified for deep and learned study but who earnestly desire to be truly devoted to God.

Within these common explanations, unprejudiced readers will find a hidden inspiration that will stir them to seek that happiness that all should want to enjoy.

In asserting that holiness is easy to attain, I use the word "easy" because it is indeed easy to find God when we seek him within ourselves. Some might quote the passage in John that says, "You will seek me, but you will not find me." This apparent stumbling block is removed, however, by another passage where Jesus, who cannot contradict himself, has also said, "Seek and you will find." It is true that those who seek God but are unwilling to give up their sins will not find God because they seek him where he cannot be found. That is why Jesus adds, "You will die in your sins." However, those who take

Preface

the trouble seek God in their hearts, sincerely abandoning their sins in order to draw closer to him, will always find him.

A life of devotion seems so overwhelming, and the spirit of prayer so difficult to attain, that many people are discouraged from taking a single step towards it. However, the presumed difficulties of any undertaking often cause despair of success and reluctance to begin, so the desirability of this undertaking and the idea that is easy to accomplish should compel you to begin this pursuit with pleasure and pursue it with energy. The advantages and ease of this method are thus set forth in this book.

If people could only be convinced of the goodness of God toward his poor creatures and of his desire to share himself with them, they would not imagine dreadful obstacles or be so easily discouraged from obtaining the goodness that he is so earnest to give them. As it's written, "He who didn't spare his own son but gave him up for our sake—how will he not, with his son,

A Short and Easy Method of Prayer

freely give us everything?" Could God refuse us anything? Certainly not! It only takes a little courage and perseverance. People have both when it comes to worldly matters, but they have none at all when it comes to "the one thing that is necessary."

If anyone thinks that God is not easily found in this method of simple love and pure obedience, they don't need to change their minds because of my testimony. However, let them try this method for themselves. Their own experience will convince them that the reality far exceeds my descriptions of it.

Beloved reader, please read this little book with a sincere and honest spirit, with a humble mind, and not with an inclination to quibble or attack. You will reap some level of benefit from it. It was written with a heartfelt desire that you might wholly devote yourself to God. Receive it, then, with a similar desire for your own holiness. Its purpose is simply to offer you a simple and childlike method for approaching your father,

Preface

who delights in the humble trust of his children and is grieved at their distrust. With sincere desire to leave sin behind, then, seek nothing from this unpretentious method but the love of God, and you will undoubtedly find it.

I do not at all claim that my opinion is better than those of others. I simply mean to explain, based on my own experience and the experience of others, the happy benefits of following the Lord in this way.

Because this book was only meant to teach about prayer, nothing is said about many other things that I value because they do not relate directly to prayer. However, as long as this book is read in the spirit in which it has been written, then without a doubt, you will find nothing shocking or troubling. And even more certainly, if you earnestly try this method, you will see for yourself that I have written the truth.

It is you alone, blessed Jesus, who loves simplicity and innocence and "whose delight is to dwell with the children of men," with those who are willing to become your "little children"—it is you alone who can make this little book valuable by using it to speak to the hearts of those who read it, leading them to seek you within themselves, where you rest like in the manger, waiting there to receive little tokens of their love and to give them proof of yours. They may still deprive themselves of these good things, but it belongs to you—almighty child! uncreated love! silent and all-encompassing word!—to make yourself loved, enjoyed, and understood. You can do this, and I know that you will do this with this little book, which belongs entirely to you, comes entirely from you, and talks only about you.

Most gracious and beloved savior, to you be all the glory!

One

The Call to Prayer

Everyone is capable of prayer, and it's a terrible misfortune that almost everyone in the world thinks they are not called to prayer. Because God provides the strength to do this, everyone is called to prayer, just as everyone is called to salvation.

Prayer is simply the heart turning toward God and the inner practice of love. Paul tells us to "pray without ceasing." Jesus tells us to "watch and pray." Everyone, then, can and should pray. I grant you that meditation is only attained by a few because few are capable of it. That is not the kind of prayer that God requires from you, and it is not the kind of prayer that I am writing about here.

A Short and Easy Method of Prayer

Everyone should pray. You must live in prayer, just as you live in love. As Jesus says, "I counsel you to buy from me gold that's been tried in the fire so that you will be rich." This is easy to obtain, much easier than you imagine.

Come, you who are thirsty, and drink the water of life. Don't lose any time by carving out "broken cisterns that can hold no water." Come, you hungry souls, who find nothing that satisfies you, and you will be filled. Come, you suffering ones, bent beneath your burden of pain, and you will be comforted. Come, you sick ones, to the great physician. Don't be scared to approach him because you're filled with disease. Show him your diseases, and he will heal them.

Come, children. Draw near to your father, and he will embrace you with arms of love. Come, you poor, wandering sheep. Return to your shepherd. Come, sinners, to your savior. Come, you unlearned ones who think you're least capable of prayer. You are more particularly called to it and ready for it. Come, everyone, without exception.

The Call to Prayer

Jesus himself calls you all to prayer!

Only those who have no heart are excused. There must be a heart before there can be love. But who really has no heart? Oh, come and give that heart to God! Come to the place of prayer and learn how to do it.

All those who long for prayer can easily pray. They are enabled by the graces and gifts of the Holy Spirit that are given to everyone.

Prayer is the key to Christian holiness and the highest good. It is the way to be rid of every vice and acquire every virtue. The one great method to become holy is to walk in the presence of God. He himself says, "Walk before me and be holy." Prayer alone brings you into his presence and keeps you there without interruption.

You must learn a type of prayer that can be used at all times and doesn't get in the way of external work. This prayer can be practiced by anyone—princes, kings, priests, judges, soldiers, children, artisans, laborers, women, and the sick. It is not a prayer of the mind but of the heart.

A Short and Easy Method of Prayer

Because the mind is so limited, it's only able to think about one thing at a time. The prayer of the heart is not interrupted by the workings of the mind. Nothing can interrupt the prayer of the heart except for unruly emotions, and once you've tasted God and the sweetness of his love, you will find it impossible to delight in anything but God himself.

Nothing is so easily obtained as the possession and enjoyment of God. He is more present to you than you are to yourself. He desires to give himself to you more than you desire to receive him. You only need to know how to seek him, and the way is easier and more natural to you than breathing.

You who think that you are so dull and fit for nothing, through prayer you can live in God himself with less difficulty or interruption than you have living in life-giving air. Isn't it then a great sin for you to neglect prayer? However, you will surely not neglect prayer after you've learned this method, which is the easiest in the world.

Two

The First Level of Prayer

There are two way to bring the soul into prayer, and these should be pursued for some time. One is meditation, and the other is reading accompanied by meditation.

Meditative reading is the selection of some practical or contemplative truth—usually preferring the practical—and reading it in the following way. First, with whatever truth you have chosen, read only a small portion of it. Try to taste and digest it, to extract the essence and substance of it. Go no further as long as you're able to savor and delight in the passage. Then pick up your book again and proceed to the next portion, rarely reading more than a half page at a time.

A Short and Easy Method of Prayer

It's not how much you read but the way you read that yields benefits. Those who read quickly reap no more benefits than a bee would reap by skimming over the surface of a flower instead of penetrating into the flower and extracting its sweetness. Broad reading is better suited for academic subjects than spiritual truths. To reap benefits from spiritual books, you must read as I've explained. I'm confident that if you practice reading slowly like this, you'll slowly become used to praying through your reading and inclined toward this practice.

Meditation should be done at a different, set time and not in the time given to reading. I believe the best way to meditate is as follows.

First, when you are brought into the presence of God through an act of faith, read something of substance and from it gather some truth that provides food for you. Pause gently on that truth, not to analyze it but to use it as a way to focus your mind. Your main practice is to be in the presence of God, so reading should be done

The First Level of Prayer

to help you collect your thoughts, not to exercise your mind.

Next, let an active faith that God is directly present in your innermost soul produce in you an eager sinking into yourself, restraining all your senses from wandering. This helps you to extract yourself from numerous distractions and then to draw close to God, who can only be found in your innermost center, the holy of holies in which he dwells. He has promised that if you keep his commandments, he will come to you and make his home with you. Augustine judges himself for all the time he lost by not first seeking God in this way.

You have now fully entered into yourself and are warmly penetrated throughout with a living awareness of God's presence. Your senses are all collected, withdrawn from the outward things and brought to your center. Your soul is sweetly and silently given to the truths you have read—not through studying them but through feeding on them, enlivening the will

A Short and Easy Method of Prayer

with emotions rather than tiring the mind with study. When your emotions are in this state—which, however difficult it may appear, is easily attained—you must allow your heart to rest quietly and peacefully and, as it were, to swallow what it has tasted.

People may enjoy the flavor of the finest food by chewing, but they receive no nourishment unless they swallow the food. In the same way, if you continually stir up the heart once it has been kindled, you will extinguish its fire and deprive the soul of its nourishment. You should therefore swallow the blessed meal that you've received with a loving rest, full of respect and confidence. This method is quite necessary. It advances the soul more quickly in a short time than other methods do in years.

Although I have said that your immediate and primary work should be to contemplate the presence of God, you also need to diligently recall your wandering senses. That is the easiest way to overcome distractions. People who try

The First Level of Prayer

to oppose distractions directly only irritate and increase them. By sinking within yourself and enjoying a sense by faith of a present God, you regather your senses and unconsciously wage a successful but indirect war with distractions.

It is proper here for me to caution beginners against wandering from truth to truth and from topic to topic. The right way to enter deeply into every divine truth, to enjoy its full delight, and to imprint it on your heart is to dwell on it for as long as it remains flavorful.

It is difficult at first to gather yourself like this because of your soul's natural habit of paying attention to outward things. However, after the soul struggles a little to get used to it, the process soon becomes quite easy. This is partly from the force of habit and partly because God, whose one desire towards his creatures is to give himself to them, provides abundant grace and the experience of enjoying his presence. That is what makes it easy.

Three

Prayer without Reading

Those who do not read are not excluded from prayer because of that. The great book, which teaches all things and can be read inwardly as well as outwardly, is Jesus himself. If you don't read, then you should use the following method.

First, you must learn this fundamental truth, that "the kingdom of God is within you." It is there, but you must seek it.

Ministers should teach their parishioners about prayer just as they do about theological truth. They teach their parishioners about the purpose of their creation. Shouldn't they also give them sufficient instructions about how they may attain it? They should teach them to begin

Prayer without Reading

by an act of deep worship and humility before God. Closing their physical eyes, they should open the eyes of their souls. They should collect themselves inwardly and, through a living faith in the God who lives within them, enter into his divine presence, not allowing their senses to wander away but keeping them focused on God as much as they can.

The second thing to do is to repeat the Lord's Prayer in your native language: "Our father, who is in heaven, holy be your name." Consider the meaning of these words and the infinite willingness of the God who dwells within you to indeed become your father. In this place, pour out your desires before him. After you pronounce that endearing word "father," stay there for a moment in respectful silence, waiting to have the will of your heavenly father revealed to you.

Look upon yourself as a helpless child, bruised by repeated falls, dirty, and without the strength to continue or the ability to clean yourself. Lay your miserable situation before the

A Short and Easy Method of Prayer

father in your humility. Breathe out a few words of love and sorrow, and then rest before him in deep silence.

Continue the Lord's Prayer: "Your kingdom come." Ask this king of glory to reign over you, yielding to the claim his love has over you and committing yourself entirely to his divine oversight. If you feel an inclination to remain in stillness and silence, stay there for as long as this feeling remains without continuing with the prayer.

When the feeling subsides, continue to the next petition: "Your will be done on earth as it is in heaven." With these words, ask God to accomplish his will in you and through you. Surrender your heart and your freedom into his hands to do with as he pleases. Understanding that the best work of his will is to love, you should desire to love God with all your strength and ask him for his pure love. However, do this quietly and peacefully.

Continue in this way through the rest of this prayer that you've been taught. However,

Prayer without Reading

don't burden yourself with frequent repetitions of prayers like this. With the Lord's Prayer, repeating it once in the way I've described will produce abundant fruit.

At other times, you should place yourself before God as a sheep before your shepherd, looking up to him for your true food: "Divine shepherd, you feed your flock with yourself. You are indeed my daily bread." You may also tell him about the needs of your family, but you should do so based on this one principle and within this one great vision of faith — that God is within you.

You may imagine Jesus as crucified, or a child, or in some other part of his human life as long as your soul always looks toward these images in its innermost center. However, you should not try to create any images of God the Father. The ideas we form about the divine being fall infinitely short of what he actually is. A living faith in his presence is sufficient.

At other times, you may look to God as a sick person looks to a doctor, bringing your illnesses to him so that he can heal you. However, this too must be done without a struggle and with silence from time to time so that the silence will be mingled with the words. Gradually, lengthen the silence and shorten the spoken prayer so that as you yield to the workings of God, his work gains the upper hand.

When God gives his presence to you and you gradually begin to enjoy silence and rest, your experience of the presence of God introduces your soul to the second level of prayer. This second level can be attained by nonreaders as well as scholars. Indeed, some favored souls are given it from the beginning.

Four

The Second Level of Prayer

Some call the second level of prayer "contemplation," the prayer of faith and stillness. Others call it "the prayer of simplicity." That is the term I will use. It's more appropriate than "contemplation," which is a more advanced level of prayer than the one I discuss here.

After the soul has practiced the first level of inward-focused prayer for some time, it finds itself gradually more able to approach God with ease. Staying focused on God becomes less difficult. Prayer becomes easy, sweet, and delightful. The soul knows that this is the true way of finding God and feels that "his name is like ointment poured out." However, your

A Short and Easy Method of Prayer

method of prayer must now change, and what I prescribe should be followed with courage and faith, without being shaken by any difficulties you may encounter.

First, as soon as the soul by faith places itself in the presence of God and gathers itself before him, it should remain in an attitude of deep and respectful silence for a time.

However, if at the beginning of this act of faith, the soul feels a pleasing sense of the divine presence, let it remain there without troubling itself about anything. Proceed no farther. Carefully cherish this experience as long as it continues. As it subsides, the will may be stirred by some delicate feeling. If the soul then finds itself reinstated in peace, let it stay there. The smothered fire must be gently fanned. However, as soon as the fire is kindled, you have to stop fanning the fire or you will put it out with your own efforts.

I warmly recommend that you never leave your time of prayer without remaining in a

The Second Level of Prayer

respectful silence for a while. It is also important for the soul to go to prayer with courage and a pure and disinterested love that seeks nothing from God except for the ability to please him and to do his will. Servants who only fit their work to the reward they expect make themselves unworthy of any reward.

Go to prayer, then, not to enjoy spiritual delights but to be either full or empty—as God chooses. This will preserve you with a steady spirit as you go through times of barrenness and times of abundance. It will keep you from being taken aback by times of dryness or the apparent rejections of God.

Five

Spiritual Droughts

God has a strong desire is to give himself to the loving soul who seeks him. However, he often hides himself in order to wake the soul from sleep and force it to seek him with love and faithfulness. How well he then rewards the faithfulness of his beloved with abundant goodness. His apparent withdrawal from you is followed by consoling caresses of love.

During these times of spiritual drought, you may believe that you will be able to prove your faithfulness and prevail over your emotions if you seek God from your own strength and through your own efforts. You may also think that doing this will in some way force God

Spiritual Droughts

to return to you more quickly. No, my dear soul, no. Please believe me, that is not the right thing to do at this second level of prayer. With a patient love, with great humility, with the steady breathing of passionate yet peaceful affection, and with a most respectful silence, you must simply wait for the return of your beloved.

Only in this way do you show him that it is him alone that you love, that you care about his pleasure, not the pleasure that you find in loving him. As it is written, "Do not be impatient in the time of clouds. Suffer the suspension and delays of God's consolation. Cling to God, wait patiently for him, and endure so that your life may be increased afterwards."

Be patient in prayer. Even if you do nothing for the rest of your life but wait for the return of your beloved, be patient. Wait with deep humility, calm contentment, and patient resignation to his will. This excellent prayer often includes the sighs of grieving love. It pleases the heart of Jesus, and moves him to return more than anything else.

Six

Abandonment

At this level of prayer, you must begin to abandon your whole existence to God. You do so because of the strong and absolute conviction that everything that happens in every moment is what he wills and allows, that it is exactly what your situation requires. This conviction makes you content with everything. It makes you see everything that happens from God's perspective and not your own.

However, my beloved, if you sincerely desire to give yourself to God, I beg you to remember that once you have given yourself away, you may not take yourself back. Once you've given something away, it is no longer at your disposal.

A Short and Easy Method of Prayer

Abandonment is a matter of the greatest importance in your progress. It is the key that unlocks the inner sanctuary. Those who truly know how to abandon themselves soon find holiness. You must therefore continue steadfastly and resolutely in this without listening to the voice of human reason. Great faith produces great abandonment, so you must trust God entirely, believing "hope against hope."

Abandonment means throwing aside all concern for yourself so that you are entirely at God's disposal. All Christians are urged to abandonment. As it's written, "Don't think about tomorrow. Your heavenly father knows you need all these things." And, "In all your ways, acknowledge him, and he will direct your paths." And again, "Give your works to the Lord, and your plans will be established." And finally, "Give your future to the Lord. Trust him. He will make it happen."

Your abandonment, then, should to be a complete giving away of all your concerns, both

Abandonment

outwardly and inwardly, putting them into the hands of God, forgetting yourself and thinking only of God. In this way, your heart remains disengaged, free, and at peace.

You practice abandonment by continually giving your will to the will of God. You renounce all your natural inclinations as soon as they arise, no matter however good they may appear, so that you may stand without prejudice toward yourself and only desire what God has determined from before time. Resign yourself in all matters, whether for the body or the soul, for time or eternity. Give the past to forgetfulness, the future to providence, and the present to God. Content yourself with the present moment, which brings God's eternal plan for everyone and is as infallible as it is inevitable and true.

Don't give any credit to yourself for anything that happens to you, either. Instead, remember that all things are from God, that they come infallibly from his hand, with the only exception being your own sin. Let yourself be guided by God as he chooses in both the inward and outward life.

Seven

Suffering

Be patient with any suffering that God gives you. If you want to love him purely, you must not seek him any less on Calvary than you do on Mount Tabor. You must love him as much on Calvary as you do on Tabor because it was on Calvary that he made the greatest manifestation of his love for you.

Don't be like those who give themselves to him at one time, only to withdraw themselves later. They give themselves to be caressed, but they take themselves back when they are crucified, seeking their own comfort.

No, beloved, you will find no comfort in anything but the love of the cross and in complete abandonment. The one who doesn't love the cross doesn't love the things of God. It is impossible to love God without loving the cross, and the heart that loves the cross finds even the most bitter things to be sweet. "To the hungry soul, every bitter thing is sweet" because it is as hungry for the cross as it is for God. God gives you the cross, and the cross gives you God.

You can be assured that there is inward progress when there is progress in the way of the cross. Abandonment and the cross go hand in hand.

As soon as suffering comes to you and you want to run away from it, abandon yourself to God at once. Present yourself to him as a sacrifice. You will find that when the cross arrives, it will not be as burdensome because you have desired it. This will not prevent your experiencing of its weight, however, as some have imagined. The experience of suffering is one of the principal parts of suffering itself. Jesus himself chose to suffer it in all its intensity. Often you will bear

Suffering

the cross with weakness. At other times, you will bear it with strength. It should all the same for you, as God chooses.

Eight

Revelation

Some may object that with this method of prayer, God won't bring revelations to your mind. However, this is far from the truth. In fact, this is *how* he gives revelations to the soul. You are abandoned to Jesus. You follow him as the way, you hear him as the truth, and he enlivens you as the life.

In giving himself to your soul, Jesus imprints upon your soul all the conditions that he faced on earth. Bearing all the conditions of Jesus within your soul is much greater than simply meditating on those conditions. Paul bore the conditions of Jesus on his body. "I bear in my body," he says, "the marks of the Lord Jesus."

Revelation

He doesn't say that he merely thought about those conditions.

In this state of abandonment, Jesus frequently gives you specific understandings or revelations of the conditions of his life. You should gratefully accept these and commit yourself to whatever appears to be his will. Indeed, having no other choice but to earnestly follow him, to live in him, to sink into nothingness before him, you must receive with equal openness anything he gives you—light or darkness, fruitfulness or barrenness, strength or weakness, sweetness or bitterness, temptations or distractions, pain, weariness, uncertainty. None of these things should slow your progress for even one minute.

God employs some people in the contemplation or enjoyment of a single revelation for years. The straightforward consideration or contemplation of this truth composes the soul, so the soul should be faithful to that work. However, as soon as God sees fit to remove a revelation, the soul must willingly yield it to him.

A Short and Easy Method of Prayer

Some are deeply troubled by their inability to meditate upon divine truths, but they don't need to be. A loving attachment to God includes within itself every kind of devotion. Whoever is peacefully united to God is excellently and effectively connected to every divine truth. Whoever loves God loves everything about him.

Nine

Virtue

This method of prayer is a short and sure way of building character. Because God is the source of all virtue, you take hold of all virtue in taking hold of God. To the degree that you abandon yourself to him, you receive the highest virtues.

Unless virtue is given inwardly, it is just a mask, an outward appearance that can be changed as easily as your clothes. When virtue is given inwardly, it is true, essential, and permanent. As David says, "The King's daughter is all glorious within." These souls, more than any others, practice virtue to the highest degree—even though they don't focus on any one particular virtue. God, to whom they are united, leads them to the

A Short and Easy Method of Prayer

broadest practice of virtue. He guards them jealously and allows not even the smallest worldly pleasure.

How these souls glow with divine love, hungry for suffering! How they would fling themselves into extreme austerity if they were allowed to follow their own inclinations. They think of nothing but how to please their beloved. As their self-love decreases, they neglect and forget themselves. As their love for God increases, so they detest themselves and disregard the creature.

If everyone would learn this simple method of prayer, which is so available to everyone, from the most ignorant to the most learned, how easily the whole church of God would be reformed. You only need to love. Augustine says, "Love, and then do as you please." When you truly love God, you won't want to do anything that might displease to your beloved.

Ten

Subduing the Body

Aside from inward contemplation, it is next to impossible to ever subdue the senses and desires of the body. The reason is obvious. The soul gives life and energy to the senses, and the senses stir up the body's desires. A dead body has neither sensations nor desires because its connection to the soul is dissolved.

All attempts to merely correct the outward life with physical discipline force the soul even further outward into this world that attracts it so powerfully. The powers of the soul are scattered. By engaging in physical disciplines and other outward acts, the soul invigorates the very senses it is trying to subdue. The senses have no

A Short and Easy Method of Prayer

other source of energy than their connection to the soul. Their activity is directly proportional to the attention the soul gives them. The activity of the senses stirs the desires of the body instead of subduing them. Physical disciplines may indeed weaken the body, but for those reasons, they can never remove the sharpness of the senses or lessen their activity.

The only way to subdue the body is through a contemplation that turns the soul entirely inward to take hold of the present God. When the soul directs all its energy towards this center of its being, this simple act separates and withdraws the soul from the senses. The inward use of the soul's energy leaves the senses weak and faint. The closer the soul draws to God, the farther it moves away from the senses and the less the senses stir the passions of the body. Those in whom the attractions of grace are powerful find that the physical person is altogether weak, powerless, and even prone to fainting.

Subduing the Body

I don't mean to discourage physical discipline. It should always accompany prayer, according to your strength and condition, or as obedience allows. However, physical discipline should not be your main work. You shouldn't give yourself this or that outward deprivation, either, but should simply follow the inward leadings of grace. When you are possessed and directed by the presence of God, he himself will enable you to do any kind of physical discipline without your having to think about it. He will give no rest to those who dwell in him until he has subdued everything that needs to be subdued.

Therefore, you only need to steadily give your utmost attention to God, and all outward discipline will be done correctly. Not everyone is capable of outward deprivations, but everyone is capable of this. In disciplining the eye and ear, which continually supply the busy imagination with new objects, there is some danger of falling into distraction. However, God will teach

A Short and Easy Method of Prayer

you this, too. You only need to follow where his Spirit guides you.

The soul has a double advantage by proceeding in this way. By withdrawing from outward objects, it draws nearer to God, and by drawing nearer to God, it receives secret sustaining and preserving power and virtue. The nearer it comes to God, the farther it is removed from sin so that its divine transformation becomes habitual.

Eleven

Conversion

As it is written, "Turn to the one from whom the children of Israel have so deeply rebelled." Conversion is simply a matter of turning away from the creature in order to return to God. Conversion is not complete when it is only an outward turning away from sin to grace. That is good and necessary for salvation, but to be complete, conversion must take place inwardly.

Once the soul turns toward God, it finds a surprising ability to remain turned toward him. The longer the soul remains turned toward God, the closer it comes to God and attaches itself to him. The closer the soul comes to God, the farther it moves away from the creature because the creature is so opposed to God. In this way, the soul is so effectively established and rooted in its conversion that being turned toward God becomes habitual—even natural.

Don't suppose that this can be done though any vigorous effort from your own powers. You are not capable of and should not attempt any partnership with divine grace other than to withdraw yourself from outward objects and turn inward. After that, there is nothing to do except continue firmly in obedience to God.

God has an attractive quality that draws the soul more and more powerfully to himself. In drawing the soul toward himself, he purifies it. He does this in the same way that the sun draws mist from the ground. As the mist slowly rises, the sun burns it off and thus makes it pure. The mist contributes nothing to this process except its own passivity, but the soul cooperates freely and voluntarily.

This kind of inward turning toward God is easy, and it moves the soul forward naturally

Conversion

and without effort because God is the center of the soul. The center always has always a strong, attractive quality. The higher and more spiritual the center is, the more forcefully and irresistibly is its attraction.

In addition to the attractive power of the center, every creature has a strong inclination to reunite with its center. This is as powerful and active as the center is spiritual and perfect.

As soon as anything turns toward its center, it falls toward it with great speed unless some invincible obstacle holds it back. A stone held in the hand is no sooner dropped than it falls by its own weight to the earth, which is its center. In the same way, unless they are held back by some object, fire and water flow incessantly towards their centers. Once the soul is turned toward its center by inward reflection, it too falls gradually, without any weight except for the weight of love, into its proper center. The more passive and peaceful it remains, free from self-advancement, the more rapidly it falls because the attraction of

A Short and Easy Method of Prayer

the center is not obstructed and has full permission to act.

You should thus give all your attention to acquiring the highest level of inward focus. You shouldn't be discouraged by the difficulties you encounter in this practice, either, because God will soon reward your practice with such abundant grace that it will become easy. You must only be faithful in meekly withdrawing your heart from outward distractions and occupations and turning toward to your center with tenderness and serenity.

If at any time turbulent outward desires arise, a gentle, inward retreat toward God will deaden them. Any other resistance to those desires will only stir them up more.

Twelve

The Third Level of Prayer

The soul that is faithful in the practice of love and obedience to God that I've described will be astonished to feel him gradually taking possession of the whole being. The soul now enjoys a continual sense of God's presence as if it were born to it. Like prayer, this is the result of habit. The soul feels an unusual serenity gradually spreading over it. Its prayer is all silence. God gives love directly to the soul, and so begins an unspeakable happiness. If I could only describe the infinite stages that follow! However, because I am writing for beginners, I must stop here and wait for God to bring to light what's useful for those who are more advanced.

A Short and Easy Method of Prayer

It is a matter of the highest importance that you stop doing anything on your own so that God may act on his own. As David writes, "Be still, and know that I am God." However, people are so infatuated with love and so invested in their own efforts that they can't believe they are working at all unless they can feel, discern, and understand what they are doing. They don't understand that the speed of God's work prevents them from seeing the details of their own progress and that as God's work becomes more abundant, his work absorbs their works.

The sun absorbs the light of the stars as it rises. It's not the lack of light but the abundance of light that keeps you from seeing the stars during the day. In the same way, you no longer perceive your own efforts because God's strong light absorbs all your small, distinct lights and makes them fade away entirely.

Those who claim that this level of prayer is merely idleness are greatly deceived. They claim this because of their lack of experience. If they

The Third Level of Prayer

would only try to reach this level themselves, they would soon become full of light and knowledge about it. The appearance of inaction doesn't come from a scarcity but abundance. The experienced soul will recognize that the silence is filled and made holy by God's activity.

There are two types of people who keep silent. One type has nothing to say. The other type has too much to say. At this level of prayer, it is the latter type of silence. The silence comes from abundance, not scarcity.

Water causes death in two very different ways. One death is dying of thirst, the other is drowning. One person dies from scarcity, and the other dies from abundance. In the same way, the fullness of God's grace now stills your natural efforts. This is why it's so important for you to remain as silent as possible.

A nursing infant is another vivid illustration. The infant begins to draw the milk by moving its tiny lips. When the milk begins to flow abundantly, the child is content to swallow without

A Short and Easy Method of Prayer

effort. Doing anything else will cause the child to harm itself, to spill the milk and force the child to quit the breast.

You must do the same at the beginning of prayer by moving the lips of your own expressions of love. However, as soon as the milk of grace begins to flow freely, you have nothing to do but to remain still, to drink it pleasantly, and when it stops flowing, to again stir up your love like the infant moving its lips. Any other activity doesn't make the best use of this grace, which is given to draw the soul into the stillness of love rather than the many expressions of self.

Who would believe that this child who gently and without effort drinks the milk could receive any nourishment? However, the more peacefully the infant feeds, the better it thrives. What happens next? The baby gently falls asleep at its mother's breast. In the same way, the soul that is still and peaceful in prayer regularly sinks into a mystic slumber. All its natural abilities are silenced, and over time, this temporary peace

The Third Level of Prayer

becomes its permanent condition. The soul is thus led forward without problems, effort, study, or craft.

Your inward being is not a fortress that must be taken with cannons and violence. It is a kingdom of peace that is only acquired by love. If you follow the little path that I have pointed out, it will lead you to this level of infused prayer. God requires nothing extraordinary and difficult here. On the contrary, he is the most pleased with childlike simplicity.

The greatest accomplishments of religion are those that are the easiest to reach. The most essential rules are the least difficult. It is the same with worldly things. Do you want to go to the sea? Set out on a river, and without effort or planning, the river will take you to the sea. Do you want to go to God? Follow this pleasant and simple path, and you will arrive at your destination with an ease and speed that will amaze you.

If you will only try it once! How soon you'll find that everything I've said is too limited and

A Short and Easy Method of Prayer

that your own experience will carry you far beyond it. What are you afraid of? What keeps you from instantly throwing yourself into the arms of love that Jesus stretched out on the cross so that he could embrace you? What risk is there in trusting God entirely and abandoning yourself to him? He will not deceive you—except perhaps by giving you far more than you ever expected!

On the other hand, those who expect to accomplish everything for themselves may hear the reproach that God gives through Isaiah: "You became weary on your many journeys, but you did not say, 'Let us rest in peace.'"

Thirteen

The Presence of God

The soul that has come this far needs only to remain still. The presence of God during the day, which is the primary result of prayer, or prayer itself, now begins to be almost continually infused into the soul. The soul enjoys transcendent blessings and finds that God is more intimately present to the soul than the soul is to itself.

The only way to find God is by turning inward. As soon as your eyes close, your soul finds itself wrapped in prayer. The soul is amazed at such a great blessing. It enjoys an inward conversation that outward matters cannot interrupt.

As Solomon said of wisdom, so you might say about this way of praying: "All good things come to me with her." Virtues flow naturally from the soul into practice, and with so much pleasure and ease they seem natural. The living spring within the soul flows out abundantly into an easy capacity for everything good and an unawareness of everything evil.

Let your soul then remain faithful in this condition. Beware of choosing or seeking any other frame of mind as preparation for confession or communion, action or prayer. The soul's only business now is to expand itself for the full reception of the divine presence. Don't misunderstand me. I am not talking about the outward preparations that are necessary for the sacraments but about the best frame of mind in which they can be received.

Fourteen

Inward Silence

As Habakkuk says, "The Lord is in his holy temple. Let all the earth be silent before him." Inward silence is absolutely necessary because for Jesus to be received into the soul, the soul must be in a frame of mind that corresponds to who he is — the eternal and essential Word.

Hearing is the sense that receive sounds, and it is passive rather than active, receiving but not sending sounds. If you want to hear, you must use your ears for that purpose. In the same way, the eternal Word — without whose divine speech the soul is dead, dark, and barren — requires your most silent attention to his enlivening and powerful voice when he has something to say.

A Short and Easy Method of Prayer

This is why the scriptures so often tell you to listen to God and pay attention to his voice. I could quote many passages but will mention only a few: "Listen to me, my people. Give ear to me, my nation." And, "Listen to me, house of Jacob and all the remnant of the house of Israel." And also, "Listen, daughter, and consider, and give ear to me. Forget your own people and your father's house, and the king will greatly desire your beauty."

You must forget yourself and all self-interest. You must listen and pay attention to God. These two simple actions—or rather, passive attitudes—give birth to a love for the beauty that he shares with you.

Outward silence is necessary for the cultivation and refinement of inward silence. Indeed, it's impossible to acquire inward silence without having a love for outward silence and solitude. As God says through his prophet Hosea, "I will bring her into the wilderness, and there I will speak to her heart." It is impossible to be inwardly

Inward Silence

occupied with God and outwardly occupied with countless trifles.

When through dullness or unfaithfulness you become distracted—that is, uncentered—it's essential that you gently and pleasantly turn inward again. In this way, you can learn to preserve the spirit of prayer throughout the day. If your prayer is confined to an appointed hour or half-hour, you reap very little fruit.

Fifteen

Confession

Self-examination should always come before confession, and the nature and method of self-examination should fit the condition of each soul. If you have arrived at this level of prayer, your work is to open your entire soul to God, who will not fail to enlighten you and enable you to see the specific nature of you faults. This examination, however, must be done in peace and stillness. You should depend on God rather than your own scrutiny to uncover and understand the nature of your sins.

When you hold yourself back from full self-examination and examine yourself by your own power, you can be easily deceived and betrayed

Confession

by self-love, calling "evil good and good evil." However, when you fully expose yourself before the sun of righteousness, his divine sunlight makes even the smallest specks of dust visible. It follows, then, that you must abandon your soul entirely to God in self-examination as well as confession.

When you reach this level of prayer, no fault escapes notice. No sooner do you sin than you feel an inward shame and painful disorder. This is the scrutiny that comes from God, who allows no evil to remain hidden. Under his purifying influence, the only thing to do is turn affectionately to your judge and bear the pain and correction he gives you with meekness.

As God becomes the incessant examiner of your soul, your soul can no longer examine itself. If you remain faithful in this abandonment, experience will show you that God's divine light is a thousand times more effective than by your own vigorous self-examination.

Those who walk in these paths need to understand one issue related to their confession where they are likely to err. When you begin to confess your sins, you find that instead of the regret and contrition you used to feel, love and peace now enter and gently take hold of your soul. Those who haven't been properly instructed will want to pull back from this sensation to perform an act of contrition because they have learned — and rightly so — that an act of contrition is required. What they don't understand is that by doing so, they lose the truer contrition, this infused love, which infinitely surpasses anything produced by their own efforts. This love contains all the other actions within itself as one central action, and it does so more perfectly than if the other actions were distinctly perceived and felt.

You shouldn't be worried about doing anything but accepting God's love and peace when he works so perfectly within you and for you. To hate sin in this way is to hate it as God does. The purest love is the love that comes from God's direct work in your soul. Why then should you be so eager to act on your own? You should

Confession

remain in the condition that God has given you, obedient to the instructions of Solomon: "Trust in God. Remain quiet where he has placed you."

You will also be surprised at finding it difficult to recall your sins. This, too, should not make you uneasy. First, this forgetfulness of your sins offers some proof of your purification, and at this stage of your development, that is for the best. Second, whenever you're called to confession, God never fails to expose your greatest sins because when he himself examines the soul, the soul sees itself more clearly than it ever could have through its own efforts.

These instructions, however, are in no way suitable for the earlier levels of prayer that require the soul to be outwardly active. In those levels, it's proper and necessary for the soul to work hard in all things according to the level of its progress. For those who have arrived at this advanced level of prayer, I encourage you to follow these instructions and not to do anything different, even when you approach communion.

A Short and Easy Method of Prayer

You should remain in silence and allow God to work freely and without restriction. Who is more ready to receive the body and blood of Christ than the one in whom the Holy Spirit resides?

Sixteen

Reading and Spoken Prayers

If you feel yourself drawn inward while reading, set aside the book and remain still. At all times, you should only read a little, and you should stop reading whenever you're drawn inward in this way.

The soul that is called into a state of inward silence should not burden itself with spoken prayers. When you pray out loud and find it difficult to continue or find yourself drawn toward silence, hold back from speaking further and yield to that inward attraction — unless the repetition of these prayers is a matter of obedience to those in authority over you. In any other case, it is much better to not be burdened with

A Short and Easy Method of Prayer

or tied down to the repetition of set prayers and instead to be given entirely to the leading of the Holy Spirit. In this way, every type of outward devotion is fulfilled to the highest degree.

Seventeen

Requests

You should not be surprised at finding yourself unable to submit the same requests to God that you used to make freely and easily. Now the Spirit intercedes on your behalf according to the will of God. As Paul says, "The Spirit helps us in our weakness. We don't know how to pray as we should, but the Spirit himself intercedes for us with groaning too deep for words." You must now cooperate with God and his plans. God tends to remove all of your own plans so that his can take their place.

Allow this to happen within yourself. Don't allow yourself to remain committed to anything else, however good it may appear. It's no longer good if it in any way turns you away from what God chooses for you. What God wills for you is preferable to all other things. Shake off all commitment to your own self-interest and live on faith and submission to God. This is where genuine faith truly begins to operate within you.

Eighteen

Failings

If your soul wanders among outward things or you commit a sin, you must instantly turn inward again. Having departed from God, you must return to him as soon as possible and suffer whatever punishment that God chooses to give you.

It is important to guard against frustration when you sin. Frustration comes from the secret root of pride and the love of your own goodness. It hurts to see what you truly are. If you become discouraged by this or despair, you are all the more weakened. The distress that comes from this awareness of your failing is often worse than the failing itself.

A Short and Easy Method of Prayer

A truly humble soul is not surprised by its failings. The more it understands its own wretchedness, the more it abandons itself to God. Seeing the need it has for God's eternal strength, the humble soul pushes forward to a closer and more intimate alliance with him.

You must do the same. God himself says, "I will instruct you and teach you in the way which you should go. I will guide you with my eye upon you."

Nineteen

Temptation

A direct struggle against distraction and temptation only increases them and pulls your soul away from what should be its only occupation, remaining in the presence of God. The surest and safest way to overcome temptation is to simply turn your attention away from the evil and draw closer to God. When a little child sees a monster, it doesn't stay to fight with it. It hardly looks at it. Instead, the child races to its mother, trusting entirely in her safety. As the psalmist says, "God is in the midst of her. She will not be moved. God will help her when morning dawns."

If you do otherwise and in your weakness attempt to attack this enemy, you will usually find yourself wounded by it — if not totally defeated. However, by simply bringing yourself into the simple presence of God, you instantly find the strength you need. This is the help that David seeks: "I have set the Lord continually before me. Because he is at my right hand, I will not be shaken. Therefore my heart is glad and my tongue rejoices. My body also rests in safety." And in Exodus, Moses says, "The Lord will fight for you — you need only to be still."

Twenty

The Death of Self

Prayer is both worship and a sacrifice. According to John, it is "an incense, the smoke of which rises to God." In the Revelation of John, it says that the angel "was given much incense to offer, together with the prayers of all God's people." Prayer is the outpouring of your heart before God. As the mother of Samuel says, "I have poured out my soul before God." In the stable in Bethlehem, the prayer of the wise men at the feet of Jesus is illustrated by the incense they offer.

Prayer is the fire of love that melts, dissolves, and lifts the soul, causing it to rise to God. As the soul melts, fragrance rises from it. These sweet perfumes rise upward from the fire of the love within. This is what the bride means when she says, "While the king sits at his table, my incense sends forth its fragrance." The table is the center of the soul. When God is there and you know how to stay close to him, his sacred presence gradually dissolves the hardness of your soul. As it melts, your soul gives forth its fragrance. The bridegroom, seeing his bride thus melted by his speech, says of her, "Who is this who comes out of the wilderness, perfumed with myrrh and frankincense?"

The soul thus rises to God by giving itself up to the destructive, annihilating power of divine love. This is sacrifice that is essential in the Christian religion, and only with this sacrifice do you show true submission to the kingship of God. As it is written, "The power of the Lord is great, and he is honored only by the humble." Through the destruction of the existence of self within you, you acknowledge the supreme existence of God. Unless you cease to exist in self, the Spirit of the eternal word cannot exist in you. By giving up

The Death of Self

your own life, you give way to his coming. When you die to yourself, he lives and resides in you.

You must indeed surrender your whole being to Jesus. You must cease to live any longer in your own life so that he can become your life. As it is written, "For you died, and your life is now hidden with Christ in God." And also, "Come to me, all you who earnestly desire me." How do we come to God? We forsake and leave ourselves so that we can be lost in him, and this can only be brought about by becoming nothing. Your nothingness is the true prayer of adoration that gives to God alone "blessing, honor, glory, and power for ever and ever."

This prayer is the prayer of truth. This is what it means to "worship the Father in spirit and truth." You worship in spirit because you are drawn out of your human actions and enter into the purity of the Spirit who prays within you. You worship in truth because you are brought into the truth that is the whole of God, with nothing of the creature.

A Short and Easy Method of Prayer

There are only these two truths, the all and the nothing. Everything else is untruth. You can only honor the all of God through your own nothingness. In the moment you die to yourself, God, who will not allow you to be empty, fills you with himself.

Oh, if people could only know the virtues and blessings that come to the soul through prayer, they would never be willing to do anything else. This is the pearl of great price, the hidden treasure. Those who find it happily sell everything they own to buy it. This is the living water that springs up to everlasting life. It is the worship of God in spirit and truth, the complete performance of the gospel's teachings.

Jesus himself assures you that "the kingdom of God is within you." This is true in two ways. First, when God becomes so completely the master and lord within you that nothing of you resists his authority, your inner life becomes his kingdom. Second, when you possess God, who is the greatest good, you also possess his kingdom.

The Death of Self

There you find the fullness of joy, and there you attain the purpose of your creation. It has been said that to serve God is to reign. The purpose of your creation is indeed to enjoy God, even in this life, but alas, who truly believes that?

Twenty-one

Depending on the Spirit

Upon hearing about the prayer of silence, some people have wrongly assumed that soul remains numb, dead, and inactive. However, your soul unquestionably acts more nobly and broadly now than before it reached this level of prayer because God himself becomes the mover. Your soul moves through the working of the Holy Spirit. As Paul teaches, you should be "led by the Spirit of God."

This doesn't mean that you should stop working outwardly but that you should work through the inner guidance of his grace. This is illustrated well by Ezekiel's vision of the wheels that had a living spirit within them. Wherever

Depending on the Spirit

the spirit went, the wheels went. They ascended and descended as they were moved because the spirit of life was within them. They did not turn away as they moved. It should be the same with your soul. Your soul should be fully submitted to the will of the living Spirit who is within it, scrupulously faithful to move only as the Spirit moves. The Spirit never moves backwards to reflect upon the creature but always moves forward, pressing on towards God.

This work of the soul comes with great peace. When your soul moves at your own direction, its actions are forced and constrained, making them easier to see for what they are. When motion comes from the Spirit of grace, however, it is so free, easy, and natural that it almost seems as if you did nothing at all. As it's written, "He brought me out into a broad place. He rescued me because he delighted in me."

When your soul is inclined toward its center, or when it returns to its center through an inward gathering, its movement toward the center instantly becomes a powerful action that infinitely surpasses the speed of other types of actions. Indeed, nothing can equal the speed of this movement to the center. Although it's an action, it's so noble and peaceful, so natural and spontaneous, that the soul doesn't see how it has done anything at all.

When a wheel turns slowly, you can easily see its spokes. When it moves rapidly, you can't see them at all. In the same way, the soul that rests in God does work that is high and noble but entirely peaceful. The more peaceful it is, the swifter it moves because it is that much more given over to the Spirit that moves it and guides it. This Spirit is God himself, who in drawing you forward causes you to run to him. How well the bride understands this when she says, "Draw me toward you, and I will run after you."

Draw me toward you, my divine center, by the secret springs of my existence, and all my strength and senses will follow you! This simple drawing forward is both an ointment that heals,

Depending on the Spirit

and a perfume that attracts. As the bride says, "I follow the fragrance of your perfumes." Although the fragrance is so powerfully attractive, the soul follows it freely, without compulsion. It's as delightful as it is irresistible. As it attracts the soul with its power, it charms the soul with its sweetness. "Draw me," the bride says, and see the unity of the center that is drawn forward. "I will run after you," she says, and all the senses and powers follow the movement of the center.

Instead of promoting idleness, I promote the highest level of action by requiring a total dependence on the Spirit of God as the source of your activity. It is "in him and through him alone that you live, and move, and have your being." This humble dependence on the Spirit of God is absolutely necessary for bringing your soul back into its original unity with and simplicity before God. In doing so, your soul is able to attain the purpose for which it was created.

You must, therefore, forsake your far-ranging human activity and return to the unity and simplicity of God, in whose image people were originally created. As Solomon says, "The Spirit is one and many." His oneness does not prevent his manyness. You enter his oneness when you are united with his Spirit and have the same spirit with him. Your actions are multiplied in regard to the outward accomplishment of his will but without ever leaving this state of oneness.

When you're guided entirely by the Holy Spirit, who is infinitely active, those actions are indeed far different in energy and scope from the actions that come merely from yourself. You must yield yourself to the guidance of wisdom, "which moves more than any motion." By remaining dependent on its motion, your actions become truly productive.

As John writes, "All things were made by the Word. Nothing was created except through him." God originally made people in his own image, and he now remakes you with the Spirit of his Word, the "breath of life" that was given at creation and that contains the image of God.

Depending on the Spirit

This new life is a life of unity with God — simple, pure, intimate, and always fruitful.

Because the devil has damaged and disfigured the image of God in the human soul, the work of the same Word whose Spirit was breathed into people at creation is absolutely necessary for the renewal of the soul. Your soul can only be renewed through passive submission to the one who renews it. Who can restore the image of God within you to its original form except for the one who is the essential image of the Father?

Your work, then, is merely to put yourself into a place of openness to the work of God and to allow the Word to paint his image upon you. As long as a canvas is unsteady on its easel, the painter cannot paint an accurate image on it. In the same way, everything you do on your own makes the canvas of your soul unsteady and brings false features to the image. Your actions interrupt and hinder the work of the divine painter. You must instead remain at peace, moving only when he moves you. Jesus has life

A Short and Easy Method of Prayer

itself within himself, and he should therefore be the life of every living thing.

The spirit of the church of God is the spirit of divine action. Is the church idle, barren, or unfruitful? No. She acts, but her activity depends upon the Spirit of God, who moves and governs her. It should be the same with all her members. To be the spiritual child of the church, you must be moved by the Spirit.

Actions are judged by the greatness and dignity of their motives. This activity is undeniably the most noble because the actions produced by divine motion come directly from God. The actions of the creature, however good they may appear, are merely human — at best virtuous — even when they're done with the help of grace.

Jesus says that he has life in himself. All other beings have a borrowed life, but the Word has life in himself, and because he is able to share his life, he desires to share it with you. You must therefore give way to this life so that it can flow into you. This can only be done by the removal

Depending on the Spirit

and loss of the old life, the life of Adam and your own actions. As Paul assures you, "Anyone who belongs to Christ has become a new person. The old life is gone. A new life has begun." This condition, however, can only be established by dying to yourself and your own actions so that the actions of God can take their place.

Instead of prohibiting action, I call for it. However, you must act in absolute dependence on the Spirit of God so that his actions take the place of your own. This can only be done by bringing the creature into the Creator, and that comes from restraining yourself so that the work of God gradually becomes dominant in your life and eventually assimilates everything that belongs to you until God's work and your work are the indistinguishable.

Jesus shows us this in the gospel. Martha did the right thing, but because she did it in her own spirit, Jesus corrected her. The human spirit is restless and turbulent, and for that reason, it accomplishes very little even though it appears to do much. "Martha, Martha," Jesus says, "you are worried and upset about many things, but only one thing is needed. Mary has chosen the right thing, and it will never be taken from her." What does Mary choose? Rest, quiet, and peace. She stops doing things on her own so that the Spirit of Jesus might do things within her. She stops living her own life so that Jesus can become her life.

This is why it is so necessary for you to renounce yourself and all your own works to follow Jesus. You cannot follow him unless you are moved by his Spirit. For the Spirit to dwell within you, your own spirit must give way to him. As Paul says, "Those who are joined to Jesus have one spirit." David also says, "As for me, it is good to draw near to God. I have made the Lord God my refuge." Drawing near to God is the beginning of union with God.

Union with God has its own beginning, middle, and end. Its beginning is an inclination and attraction to God. When the soul is drawn inward as I've described, it moves into

Depending on the Spirit

the influence of its center and develops an eagerness for union. As it moves closer to God, the soul becomes connected to God, and drawing closer and closer, it becomes one spirit with him. This is when the soul that has strayed from God returns to its proper purpose.

You must now step onto this path, which is the work of God and the Spirit of Jesus. As Paul says, "Anyone who does not have the Spirit of Christ does not belong to him." To belong to Jesus, you must be filled with his Spirit. To be filled with his Spirit, you must be emptied of your own. Paul explains the necessity of this divine influence: "Those who are led by the Spirit of God are the children of God."

The Spirit of divine action is the Spirit of divine adoption, so Paul adds, "You have not received the spirit of slavery that makes you fall back into fear. You have received the Spirit of adoption that makes you cry, 'Abba! Father!'" This is the Spirit of Jesus, through whom you become his child. Paul adds, "The Spirit himself bears witness to your spirit that you are a child of God."

When you yield to the guidance of the Holy Spirit, your soul perceives the evidence of its divine adoption. It also feels—with abundant joy—that it has not received the spirit of slavery but instead the spirit of freedom, the freedom that comes with being a child of God. It finds that it can acts freely and enjoyably, with energy and certainty.

The Spirit of divine action is necessary for all things. Paul bases this necessity on our own ignorance about the thing people ask for. "The Spirit," he says, "helps us in our weakness. We don't know how to pray as we should, so the Spirit intercedes on our behalf with sighs too deep for words." This is plain enough. If you don't know what you need or how to pray for the things you need, and if the Spirit within you, to whom you've given yourself, wants to pray on your behalf, shouldn't you give him complete freedom to do his work and pray for you?

Depending on the Spirit

This Spirit is the Spirit of the Word, who is always heard. Jesus himself says, "I know that you always hear me." If you allow the Spirit within you to pray and intercede for you, you will always be heard. Why is this so? Great apostle, mystic teacher, master of the interior life, teach us why! "He who searches your hearts," Paul says, "knows the mind of the Spirit because he intercedes for the saints according to the will of God." In other words, the Spirit only demands things that conform to the will of God, and the will of God is that you should be saved and become holy. The Spirit asks for everything that is required for your holiness.

Why then should you be burdened with superficial concerns and wear yourself out with all your own activity without ever saying, "I will rest in peace"? God himself invites you to give all your concerns to him. In Isaiah, God laments—with indescribable goodness—that people use all their strength, riches, and treasure to pursue countless outward things even though

A Short and Easy Method of Prayer

there is so little joy to be found in them: "Why do you spend money on things that are not bread? Why do you labor for things that offer no satisfaction? Listen close to me! Eat what is good. Let your soul delight itself with richness."

Oh, if people only understood the blessedness of listening to God and how much the soul is strengthened by doing so! Zechariah says, "Be silent, all the world, before the Lord." All human activity must stop the moment he appears. To help you abandon yourself without reservation, God assures you through Isaiah that you have nothing to fear because he takes such special care of you: "Can a woman forget her nursing child and not have compassion on the child of her womb? Yes, even she may forget her child, but I will never forget you." Such words, so full of consolation — after hearing them, how can you fear abandoning yourself entirely to the guidance of God?

Twenty-two

The Work of the Soul

The activity of people is divided into inward or outward actions. Outward actions can be seen with the eyes and are related to some external goal. They have no moral quality except for what they receive from the inner motives behind them. In this chapter, I speak only about inward actions, those actions of the soul through which the soul turns inward toward some purposes and away from others.

If while you are guided by God, you choose to do something different, you necessarily withdraw yourself from God and turn toward a created goal, more or less according to the strength of your action. Similarly, if while you are turned toward the world, you wish to return to God, you must necessarily do something to purse that return. The more holy that action is, the more complete your return will be.

Until this conversion is complete, many repeated actions may be necessary. With some, complete conversion happens gradually over time. For others, it's instantaneous. Your work should consist of continually turning toward God, using every ability and strength of your soul purely for him. As it's written, "Reunite all the workings of your heart in the holiness of God." David says, "I will keep my whole strength for you," which you now do by earnestly re-entering into yourself. Isaiah says, "Return to your heart."

People have strayed from their hearts through sin, and God only requires the heart: "My child, give me your heart, and let your eye observe my ways." Giving your heart to God means keeping the soul always centered on him so that he can conform you to his will. You must continue steadily toward God from your very first prayer.

The Work of the Soul

Because the human spirit is unstable and in the habit of turning toward earthly things, the soul is prone to distraction. When you notice that you've strayed from God, you can resume your place in God through a simple and genuine act of returning to him. This practice continues for as long as the conversion process continues.

Because many repeated acts form a habit, the soul develops a habit of conversion. The inward activity that was interrupted earlier gradually becomes a habitual condition. You should not be perplexed, therefore, about finding your own way back to the God to whom you are already attached. You can't try to do something new on your own without great difficulty and discipline, and you may even find yourself further withdrawn from your proper place in God under the pretense of seeking something that in reality you have already acquired. That habit of attachment is already formed, and it is confirmed by continual conversion and love. You would be trying to do one action through the use of many actions instead of simply remaining attached to God alone.

At times, you may notice that you are doing many simple, outward actions that shows that you have wandered and that you need to come back into your heart after having strayed from it. Once you come back, remain there in peace. It's wrong to suppose that you shouldn't do anything—you're always doing something—but let your actions fit the level of your spiritual advancement.

The great difficulty for most spiritual people comes from not clearly understanding this issue. Some spiritual works are temporary and distinct. Others are on-going. Some are direct. Others are reflective. Not everyone can do the first, nor is everyone in the right place to do the others. The more direct actions are fitting for those who have strayed and require specific corrective works that are appropriate for how far they have strayed. If they haven't strayed far, the simplest kind of work is sufficient.

The Work of the Soul

By on-going work, I mean inward activity that always exists within God after the soul is turned toward God through a direct, outward action. This work doesn't need to be renewed unless is it's been interrupted. Once the soul is turned toward God, it remains there, abiding in love: "Those who live in love live in God." The soul exists and rests in this habitual act, but it is free from idleness because it continues in its on-going work of existing in God, of sinking gently into God, whose pull on the soul becomes more and more powerful. As it's drawn by this pull, living in love and kindness, the soul sinks continually deeper into that love, doing work now that is more powerful, vigorous, and effective than the action that first turned it back toward God.

The soul that is in this way so profoundly and vigorously active, given so entirely to God, does not notice its own activity because it is direct, not reactive. This is why some, not explaining themselves correctly, say that they do nothing.

A Short and Easy Method of Prayer

It's a mistake to say so because they have never before been so truly or nobly active. They should instead say that they don't notice their actions, not that they do nothing. I grant you that they don't act from themselves but are instead drawn toward God and follow his attraction. Love is the weight that sinks them. Someone falling down into the sea would fall from one depth to another for all eternity if the sea were infinite. In the same way, these souls, without noticing their descent, drop with unimaginable swiftness to the deepest depths.

It's incorrect, then, to say that they do nothing. Everyone does something, but the nature of those actions is different for everyone. The mistake arises from this, that those who know they should act desire to act outwardly and noticeably. However, this cannot be. Outward works are only for the beginners. There are other works for those at a more advanced stage. To remain in outward acts, which are weak and profit little, is to block yourself from the others. To attempt

The Work of the Soul

the inward work without having passed through the outward work is also a considerable error. As Solomon teaches, "To every thing there is a season." Every spiritual state has its own beginning, middle, and end, and it's an unhappy error to stop at the beginning. You can acquire no skill without making progress through the middle. At first, you struggle with hard work, but later, you reap the fruit of those labors.

When a ship is in port, the crew must exert all its strength to clear the harbor and move out to sea, but then it can move the ship with ease. In the same way, while the soul remains in sin and human nature, great effort is required to bring it into freedom. The cables that hold it must be loosened. Then with powerful and vigorous efforts, it gathers itself inward and pushes off gradually from the old port of self. Leaving that behind, it proceeds into the interior, the sea that it desires so much.

When the ship is underway, she leaves land behind according to the speed by which the

A Short and Easy Method of Prayer

crew rows her out to the sea. The farther she moves away from land, the less effort it takes to move her forward. She gets under sail and then proceeds so swiftly in her course that the oars become useless and are laid aside. The pilot is now content to spread the sails and hold the rudder.

To spread the sails is to lay yourself before God in the prayer of simple openness so that the Holy Spirit can work in you. To hold the rudder is to restrain your heart from wandering from the true course, bringing it back gently and guiding it steadily by the direction of the Spirit. The Spirit gradually gains possession and dominion over the heart, just as the wind by degrees fills the sails and moves the ship forward.

While the winds are fair, the pilot and sailors rest from their labors, and the ship glides rapidly along without their efforts. As they rest and leave the ship to the wind, they make more progress in one hour than they would have in days with their oars. If they even try to use the oars now,

The Work of the Soul

they will not only wear themselves out but also slow the ship with their poorly timed efforts.

This is the correct way to travel inwardly. Allowing God to move you forward will bring more progress in a short time than you would move through a whole life of your own repeated outward acts. Whoever tries this path will also find it the easiest path in the world.

If the wind blows against you or brings a storm, you must cast anchor to hold the ship back. This anchor is a simple confidence in God and the hope of his goodness. You must only wait patiently for the storm to pass and for a favorable wind to return. As David says, "I waited patiently for the Lord. He turned to me and heard my cry." In the same way, you must be committed to the Spirit of God, giving yourself entirely to his divine guidance.

Twenty-three

Guidance for Leaders

If all those who labor for the conversion of others tried to bring them immediately into the prayer of the inner life, making it their plan to win over the heart, then countless permanent conversions would follow. Instead, labors confined to outward things—burdening the disciple with a thousand rules for outward religious practices instead of leading the soul to Jesus through the work of the heart—brings little and only temporary fruit.

If ministers were careful to teach their parishioners this inner work, then actual shepherds would carry the Spirit of the early church as they watch their flocks, farmers at the plow would stay in holy conversation with God, builders would have renewed inner strength as they exhaust their bodies with labor. Every kind of vice would quickly disappear. Every parishioner would become a true follower of the good shepherd.

Once the heart is won, how easy it is to correct all the rest. This is why God asks for the heart above all other things. Only the conquest of the heart can uproot fearful vices that govern so many—drunkenness, profanity, lust, envy, and theft. Through the conquest of the heart, Jesus would rule everywhere in peace, and the appearance of the church would be entirely renewed.

The degradation of inward devotion is unquestionably the source of the various errors that have arisen in the church, and these errors would quickly be weakened and overcome by re-establishing inward devotion. Doctrinal errors only take root in souls that are lacking in faith and prayer. Instead of constantly arguing

A Short and Easy Method of Prayer

with these wandering parishioners, ministers should simply teach them how to believe and how to pray diligently. This would lead them gently back to God. Oh, how inexpressibly great is the loss of those who neglect the inner life! How terrifying must the day of judgment be for those entrusted with the care of souls who have not revealed and given this hidden treasure!

Some ministers excuse themselves from this work by saying that inward devotion is a dangerous path to follow or that simple people can't be taught the things of the Spirit. The word of truth says just the opposite: "The Lord loves those who walk simply." What danger can there be in walking on the only true path, which is Jesus himself? What danger can there be in giving yourself over to him, looking continually to him, placing all your confidence in his grace, and with all the strength of your soul moving toward his pure love?

Far from being incapable of this complete holiness, the openness, innocence, and humility

Guidance for Leaders

of the ordinary people makes them especially ready for and able to attain holiness. They are less distracted by their own reasoning and less committed to their own opinions. Their lack of education allows them to submit more freely to the teaching of the Holy Spirit. Those others who are confined and blinded by their independence and prejudice offer much greater resistance to the working of grace.

The scripture says that "to the simple, God gives the understanding of his law." God loves to present himself to them: "The Lord protects the simple. When I was helpless, he saved me." Spiritual fathers must not prevent their little ones from coming to Jesus. Jesus himself tells his disciples, "Leave the children alone, and don't try to keep them from coming to me because the kingdom of heaven belongs to ones like these." It was the attempt of the apostles to keep children from the Lord that brought this rebuke.

People frequently try to heal the outward body when the disease lies in the heart. The reason

A Short and Easy Method of Prayer

why the church is so unsuccessful in reforming humankind, especially those of the lower classes, is that it begins with outward matters. That work only produces temporary fruit. If the remedy for the inward life is instead given first, the outward life will be naturally and easily reformed.

This is easy to do. It's a natural and ready process to teach people how to seek God in their hearts, to think about him, to return to him when they find that they have wandered from him, to do and to endure all things with the single goal of pleasing him. It is a matter of leading their souls to the true source of grace itself, and in that grace, they find all they need for the path to holiness.

You who care for souls, I beg you to guide them onto this path, which is Jesus himself. In fact, it is Jesus himself to tells you, with the precious blood that he shed for the ones entrusted to you, to "speak to the heart of Jerusalem." Givers of his grace, preachers of his word, ministers of his sacraments—establish

Guidance for Leaders

his kingdom! To truly establish it, make him the ruler of their hearts.

The heart alone can oppose his authority, and the submission of the heart gives his authority the greatest honor: "Praise the holiness of God, and he will become your holiness." Don't teach your flock to pray through reasoning or outward forms because the simple are not capable of that. Instead, teach them the prayer of the heart, not of the mind. Teach them the prayer of God's Spirit, not prayers written by humans.

Sadly, by trying instead to teach the people elaborate, outward forms of prayer, ministers create the main obstacle to actual prayer. The children are led away from the best of fathers by language that is too refined and polished to be understood. Children, go to your heavenly Father and speak to him in your own words, however unrefined they may be. They are not unrefined to him. A father is more pleased with conversation that is disorganized by love and respect, seeing that it comes from the heart, than he is

A Short and Easy Method of Prayer

with a barren, formal speech, however elaborate it may be. The simple and undisguised emotions of a child's love are infinitely more expressive than all refined speech and all reasoning.

By creating instructions for how to love the essential Love with outward rules and formal methods, people have to a great degree estranged themselves from God. How unnecessary is it to teach an outward method for loving! The language of love comes naturally to the lover, but it is nonsense and uncivilized to the one who doesn't love. The best way to learn how to love God outwardly is to love him in the heart. The most unlearned often become the most skilled in this because they move forward with simplicity and earnestness.

The Spirit of God needs none of your plans and your outward, religious systems. Whenever it pleases him, he turns ordinary shepherds into prophets. Far from keeping anyone out of the temple of prayer, he throws open the gates so that all may enter. From the highest point in the cities, Wisdom cries out, "Let all who are simple come to my house!" To those who have no sense, she says, "Come, eat my food and drink the wine I've mixed. Leave your simple ways, and you will live." Jesus himself thanks his father for having "hidden these things form the wise and learned and revealed them to little children."

Twenty-four

Union with God

It is impossible to reach union with God solely through meditation, through the lessening of passions, or even though the highest forms of enlightened and comprehended prayer. There are many reasons for this, and the main ones are given here.

According to scripture, "No one shall see God and live." All forms of spoken prayer and even of active contemplation that are pursued as an end in themselves and not as preparation for the passive life are human works. You cannot unite with God through them. Everything comes from humans and from their works—however noble, however excellent—must first be destroyed.

Union with God

John tells us that "there was a great silence in heaven." Heaven represents the foundation and center of the soul. Before the majesty of God appears, everything in the heart must be silent. All the efforts—the very existence—of self-sufficiency must be destroyed because nothing is opposed to God except for self-sufficiency. All the evil in humans is found in this sin. It is the source of fallen human nature. The more a soul loses this quality, then, the more pure it becomes. In the end, the sinfulness of the soul that lives by its own self-sufficiency fades away as it acquires purity and innocence by abandoning the self-sufficiency that made it so unlike God.

To unite two things that are as opposed to each other as the purity of God is to the impurity of the creature, much more is required than the efforts of the creature. Nothing but the unique and powerful work of the Almighty can accomplish this because the two things must be reduced to what is common between them before they can merge and become one. Can

A Short and Easy Method of Prayer

the impurity of dross be united with the purity of gold? What then does God do? He sends his own wisdom before him, just as he will send the last fire to the earth to destroy everything that is impure. Just as nothing can resist the power of that fire, so wisdom dissolves and destroys all the impurities of the creature and prepares it for union with God.

This impurity that is so opposed to divine union is self-sufficiency and human activity. Self-sufficiency is the source of the defilement that can never be united to essential purity. The sun's rays may touch the mud, but they cannot unite with it. Human activity is opposed to divine union because God is in infinite stillness. For the soul to be united to him, it must participate in his stillness. Without stillness, there can be no union. The soul can never arrive at divine union, therefore, except through the stillness of the human will, nor can it ever be one with God except by being re-established in the purity of its first creation and in the stillness of its center.

Union with God

God purifies the soul with his wisdom in the same way that refiners purify metals with the furnace. Gold cannot be purified except by fire, which gradually consumes everything that is earthly, separating it from the gold. It's not enough for the earthly part to be blended into the gold. The gold must be melted and dissolved by the force of fire in order to separate out every earthly particle. Again and again, the gold must be put into the furnace until it loses every trace of pollution and cannot be further purified.

The goldsmith no longer finds any impurity because the gold has perfect purity and simplicity. The fire no longer changes it. Even if the gold is left in the furnace for an age, its purity will not increase and its mass will not decrease. Now it is worthy of the most exquisite workmanship.

If this gold later appears to be impure, it is an accidental impurity caused by contact with some other substance. This impurity is only superficial and doesn't affect the usefulness of the gold. This impurity is far different from its former

A Short and Easy Method of Prayer

impurity, which was hidden in the very center and foundation of its nature and identity. Those who don't understand the process of purification and its blessed effects might be inclined to reject the pure gold that has been sullied by some external impurity, preferring instead an impure metal that is superficially bright and polished.

In addition, the goldsmith cannot mix pure gold and impure gold. Before they can be united, they must be equally refined. The goldsmith therefore plunges the impure gold into the furnace until all its dross is purged and it becomes fully prepared for union with the pure gold. This is what Paul means when he says that "the fire will test the quality of everyone's work to see if it has any value." He then adds, "If your work is burned up, you lose it all. You yourself will be saved but only like someone escaping through flames." Paul suggests that there is a type of work so degraded by impurity that even though the mercy of God accepts the actions, they must pass through the fire to be purged from the self. It is

Union with God

in this sense that God is said to "examine and judge our righteousness" because "no one will be declared righteous in God's sight by the works of the law" but "righteousness is given through faith in Jesus to all who believe."

You see that divine justice and wisdom, like a pitiless and devouring fire, must destroy everything that is earthly, unspiritual, and mortal in you—along with all works of your own—before your soul is fit for and capable of union with God. This purification can never be accomplished by the works of fallen humans. On the contrary, they submit to it with reluctance because, as I have said, they are so in love with the self, so opposed to its destruction, that they always resist unless God works on them with power and authority.

You may object here that because God never robs people of their free will, people can always resist God's actions and that I err in saying that God acts unilaterally and without the consent of people.

A Short and Easy Method of Prayer

Let me explain. When people give their passive consent to God, God may assume full power and complete guidance over people without seizing control of them. In the beginning of their conversion, people unconditionally surrender themselves to everything that God chooses for them. They thus consent to whatever God might later do for them or require of them. However, when God begins to burn, destroy, and purify a person, the soul—not perceiving that these actions are meant for good and suspecting the opposite—retreats from them.

Just as gold seems to blacken rather than brighten when it's first put into the furnace, so the soul thinks that it's lost its purity and that its temptations are sins. In that moment, if an active consent were to be required, the soul could scarcely give it—and would often withhold it. The most that the soul can do in that moment is remain firm in its passive consent as well as it can, enduring the works of God that it is neither able nor willing to prevent.

Union with God

In this way, the soul is purified from all of its own distinct, perceptible, and far-ranging works, which create the great gulf between itself and God. By degrees, the soul is made obedient and then pure. The passive capacity of the creature is elevated, ennobled, and enlarged. This happens in a secret, hidden way that is called mystical, but the soul must passively agree to all of these workings. It is true, indeed, that at the beginning of this purification, the soul must work from itself. However, as the actions of God become stronger and stronger, the soul must gradually stop acting, yielding to the guidance of the Holy Spirit, until it is entirely swallowed up in the Spirit. This is often a difficult and trying process.

I do not say, then, as some suppose, that there is no need for no formal, religious devotion. On the contrary, these actions are the gate through which you enter this path. However, you should not stay there forever. You should always keep moving toward holiness, and that can't be done unless you lay aside what helped you at first.

A Short and Easy Method of Prayer

However necessary formal devotions are to at the beginning of this journey, they become a great hindrance if you cling to them obstinately. They prevent you from reaching the end. This is why Paul says, "I forget those things that are behind me, and I reach forward to those that are in front of me. I press on toward the finish line to win the prize of God's heavenly calling in Jesus."

Suppose that some people left on an important journey but then moved into the first inn along the way and called it home because they heard that many others had come that way, that some had stayed in the inn, and that the owners of the inn also lived there. Wouldn't you say that these people had taken leave of their senses? What I ask for, then, is for you to press on toward the final destination by way of the shortest and easiest road and without stopping at the first stage of the journey. May you follow the teaching and example of Paul and allow yourself to be led by the Spirit of God, which infallibly leads you to the purpose of your creation, the enjoyment of God.

Union with God

The enjoyment of God is the sole purpose for which you were created, and souls that do not have the purification of the creature and union with God in this life can only be saved as if by escaping flames. How strange it is, then, that anyone should be afraid of the process — as if the process that produces holiness and blessing in the life to come can be the cause of sinfulness and evil in the present life!

God is the highest good. The soul's essential blessedness is its union with God, and that blessedness differs among saints according to the purity of their union with God. You cannot achieve this union through your own efforts. God shares himself with your soul in proportion to its capacity. You can only be united to God in simplicity and passiveness, and because this union is itself God's blessing, the path that leads us in this passiveness cannot be evil but must be the best path and most free from danger.

This path is not dangerous. Would Jesus have made this the most perfect and necessary path if there was evil or danger in it? No! Everyone can travel on this path. Just as everyone is called to happiness, everyone is also called to enjoy God, both in this life and the next.

I say the enjoyment of God himself, too, not his gifts. His gifts do not constitute essential happiness, so they never fully satisfy the immortal spirit. The soul is so noble and great that even the highest gifts of God cannot fill its immense capacity with happiness unless the giver also gives himself to the soul. God wants to give himself to every creature according to its capacity to receive him, but how reluctant people are to allow themselves to be drawn to him. How fearful they are to be prepared for divine union.

Some say that you must not move yourself into this union with God. I grant that to them, but I also say that no one can ever do that anyway because it's not possible for anyone, through their own efforts, to unite themselves to God. He alone must do it. It is a waste of time, then, to condemn those who claim to be self-united

Union with God

because such a thing is impossible.

Some also say that people can only pretend to reach this state of union with God. I say that people cannot pretend to be united with God anymore than people dying of starvation can for any length of time pretend to be full and satisfied. Some wish or word, some sigh or expression, will inevitably escape them and betray that they are in reality far from being satisfied.

Because no one can reach union with God by their own efforts, I don't pretend to bring anyone into that union but only to point out the path that leads to it. I beg them to not be slowed down by outward practices, all of which must be abandoned when the time comes, nor to move into the first inn along the way, nor to be satisfied with the sweetness of the milk meant for babies. Experienced teachers understand this. They simply point to the Water of Life and offer their assistance to others trying to reach it. Wouldn't it be unjustifiably cruel to show a spring to thirsty people and then block them

A Short and Easy Method of Prayer

from every ever reaching it, leaving them to die of thirst? However, that is exactly what happens every day.

Let us all agree about the path just as we all agree about the destination, which is obvious and indisputable. The path has its beginning, middle, and end. The nearer you come to the end, the farther you must leave the beginning behind. It is only by moving forward that you can ever arrive at the end. It is only by leaving the one that you can arrive at the other. You can't get from the beginning to the end without passing through the middle. If the end is good, holy, and necessary, and if the beginning is also, then why should the road that leads from one to the other be considered evil?

Blind and foolish people who pride yourselves on learning, wisdom, talent, and power! How well you confirm what God has said, that he has hidden these things from the wise and circumspect and revealed them to little children.

www.ingramcontent.com/pod-product-compliance
Lightning Source LLC
Chambersburg PA
CBHW022119040426
42450CB00006B/766